Saltwater

Florida Fishes

by
Rube Allyn

Edited by Charlie Allyn

A Great Outdoors Book

Great Outdoors Publishing Co.
St. Petersburg, Florida

Foreword

Florida has a lot going for it — and a lot of people coming to it. If almost constant sunshine weren't lure enough, 4500 miles of coastline is the clincher! Actually, the straight-line distance is about 1800 miles; some experts say the coastline is over 8000 miles if you count the coastline at every island and estuary. For millions who visit the Sunshine State each year, that means packing the fishing gear along with the suntan oil. Some fish are pretty cosmopolitan; a visiting angler might pull in a Tripletail just like the one he caught back home in Connecticut — or off the coast of Spain. But there's a good chance that the finny denizen hauled into his boat will be a breed apart from those he's used to snaring. The odds increase if he hails from South Dakota.

Common names used are those approved by the American Fisheries Society. However, we have added, in some cases, local or "dockside" names. Some of these are too colorful to omit, in spite of the confusion they cause.

Consecutive numbers have been assigned to each fish in the text. These numbers appear on the color pages, and the color-page number is noted in the text where applicable.

The Editor

About the Author

The First Edition of this book was the last from the pen of Rube Allyn — he was struck down in a tragic car-bicycle accident on July 4, 1968. Nine days later, he died of the injuries suffered while on his last bicycle ride to get the evening paper.

Rube's hobby was reading newspapers. When in a strange town, nothing delighted him more than a careful and detailed perusal of the local paper. Newspapers are about people, and people fascinated Rube. He came by his interests and talents naturally; he was brought up in a succession of newspaper print shops. His father, Rube Sr., was a country editor and tramp printer whose avocation was starting newspapers in small towns and then selling out when civilization started to crowd him with too many modern conveniences. Rube Sr. ended his days a virtual hermit in Ruskin, Florida, but he still was the proud possessor of several antique printing presses and title to a quarterly magazine, *The Florida Fisherman.*

Rube Jr. was as ardent a fisherman as his father — but much more skilled. He was living proof of the old adage: "ten percent of the fishermen catch ninety percent of the fish." His interests went beyond just fishing — he wrote, set type, ran the press, and often personally delivered to the bookstores copies of his first book, *Dictionary of Fishes.* That book sold over half-million copies. When he died, he left 64 titles in print, 11 of which he authored.

Rube loved the sea, and loved to write about it. His last request was to be buried at sea — "where the Kingfishing is best." Like the evening sun, his body was swallowed by the dark waters of the Gulf of Mexico. But each day the sun rises to give new life to the creatures of the sea.

This is a Revised Edition of *Florida Fishes.* It is dedicated to the memory of Rube Allyn, Jr.

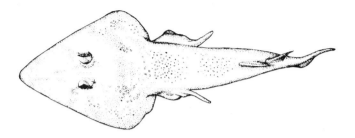

1. GUITAR FISH   *Rhinobatos lentiginosus*

Also called Fiddle Fish.

An elongated skate with narrow wings and transparent nose. Greyish-brown on top with myriad of small yellowish spots. Appears to be a missing link between a skate, a ray, and a shark.

They are occasionally caught on grassy bottom in the bays by trout fishermen.

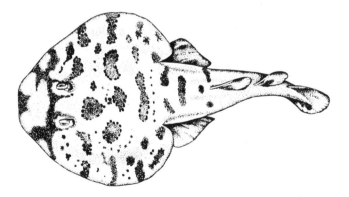

2. LESSER ELECTRIC RAY   *Narcine brasiliensis*

Also called Numbfish, Torpedo Skate.

A rounded head. Tail thicker than those of skates or other rays. Numerous dark spots over entire body. Not plentiful anywhere, but found primarily in the warm Gulf of Mexico waters, rarely to the Carolinas. Carries its own storage batteries; can give a nasty shock when touched.

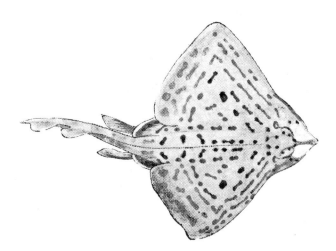

3. CLEARNOSE SKATE   *Raja eglanteria*

Also called Briar Skate.

Prettily marked with splotches of black, brown, and silver. Line of spines on back, extending onto tail. Average weight, 1 lb. Largest known, 12 lbs.

4. ATLANTIC STINGRAY   *Dasyatis sabina*

Also called Stingaree.

Olive-brown on back, whitish on lower surface. Rounded wings. Dark line and prickly spines run down the midline of the back. Average weight, 5 lbs.

The *D. americanus* or Southern Stingray, is a larger, deepwater version and seldom seen. However, a 6-foot wide, 600-lb. specimen was once caught off Bradenton Beach in Florida.

5. SPOTTED EAGLE RAY   *Aetobatus narinari*

Also called Mussel Ray, Cownose, Leopard Ray.

White belly; back is black or dark grey, with cream, white, or bluish spots. Often leaps from the water. Females said to leap when giving birth. Feeds on shellfish which they crush before skillfully extracting the insides. Average weight, 150 lbs., but known to reach 250 lbs. with a 7-foot wingspan.

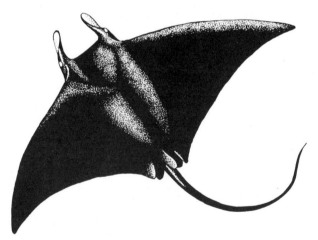

6. MANTA RAY   *Manta birostris*

Also called Devil Ray.

Black on top with white underside. Has two large flippers on each side of mouth to sweep in plankton from the surface.

While not dangerous, these fish often leap from the water to terrorize fishermen in small boats. It is an awesome sight to a fisherman in a rowboat when a 10-foot, 600-lb. Manta Ray leaps from the water, often turning a somersault and landing within an oar's length away with a load splash.

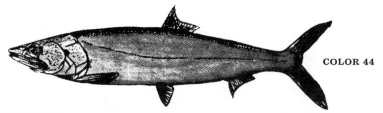

COLOR 44

7. LADYFISH   *Elops saurus*

Also called Ten Pounder, Banana Fish, Flip Flap, Big-Eyed Herring, Horse Mackerel, Bonefish, Silver King, Chiro, Skipjack Macabi.

That long list should tell you that a lot of fishermen have experienced a catch in a lot of places — a catch that should put it in the game fish class. Though easier to hook, it behaves like its large cousin, the Tarpon — and is equally poor food.

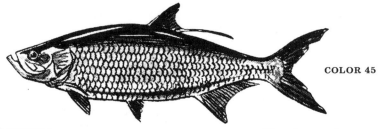

COLOR 45

8. TARPON   *Megalops atlanticus*

Also called Silverking, Silverfish, Grand Escaille, Sabalo, Savalle, Savavila, Tarpun, Camaripugucus.

To the delight of many fishermen, they "run" in Florida from late winter through early summer. One of the first marine fish to be declared a game fish, with good reason. Average length: 5 feet.

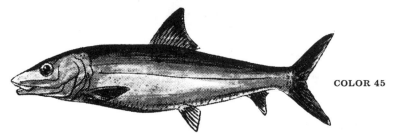

COLOR 45

9. BONEFISH   *Albula vulpes*

Also called Banana Fish, Grubber, Macabi, Silver Ghost.

Burnished silver sides which reflect sunlight like polished silver. Darker olive tinge on back.

Considered by some to be the fastest game fish, they are sought with artificial or live bait by ardent bone fishermen who pride themselves on knowing the right weight tackle and technique for the kill.

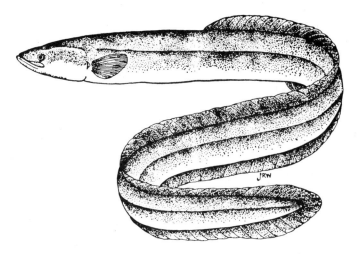

10. AMERICAN EEL   *Anguilla rostrata*

About the only discernible difference between the American and European eel is that the former has 7 fewer vertebrae. Although called "freshwater" eels, they are technically seafish, going thousands of miles out into the ocean to spawn and die. From there, the larvae head coastward to complete development in a freshwater environment. Both species have been found to intermingle where they spawn in the deep waters near the Sargasso Sea. Astonishingly, each larva knows which continent to head for.

Average length, 18 inches. Known to reach 48 inches. Food value good.

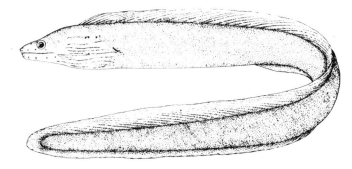

11. GREEN MORAY   *Gymnothorax funebris*

Dark green back with a yellow mucous layer on belly making it appear lighter in color. Not thought to be technically poisonous, it can inflict a nasty bite that is prone to become infected if not treated.

The Spotted Moray, the Blackedged Moray, and the Purple-mouth Moray, though less common, have been found in Florida waters.

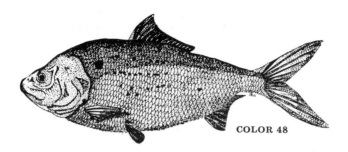

COLOR 48

12. ATLANTIC MENHADEN *Brevoortia tyrannus*

Bluish above, sides silvery with strong brassy luster.

A baitfish which is found along the Atlantic coast in great numbers in summer. They are caught with nets and used as bait and chum. Because of the strong oil content, they are ground up for chum to attract larger fish such as tuna.

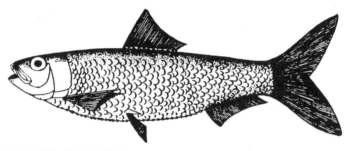

13. SCALED SARDINE *Harengula jaguana*

Silver on sides; dark green to smokey-grey on back. Belly is keeled; sharply pointed.

Numerous bait fish in southern latitudes in winter and spring. Sometimes seen as far north as Cape Cod in warm weather. Most numerous in the Florida Keys.

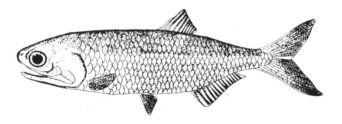

14. BAY ANCHOVY *Anchoa mitchilli*

Olivaceous with narrow silver stripe.

A bait fish, numerous around piers and in inland waters in smaller sizes. Large schools in Gulf of Mexico.

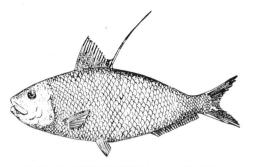

COLOR 37

15. ATLANTIC THREAD HERRING *Opisthonema oglinum*

A surface feeder, not found in large numbers. Usually found in warmer waters, although occasionally found straying north of Virginia.

Average size, 5 inches; largest 12 inches. Food value, poor.

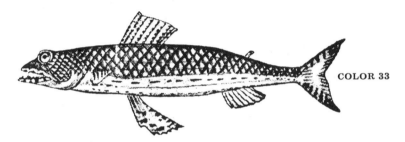

COLOR 33

16. INSHORE LIZARDFISH *Synodus foetens*

Body and sides greyish, finely mottled with brownish-green. Belly white, caudal dusky; head brownish. Eyes placed high. A mouth of formidable teeth.

A voracious feeder. Feeds on small fish, crabs, shrimp, worms, or almost anything. Cape Cod to Mexican coast and Indies.

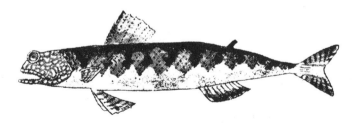

17. SNAKEFISH *Trachinocephalus myops*

Greenish on top with about ten white blotches on the side. Head is brownish. Nose rounded.

This is the smallest of the lizardfishes and most commonly taken by hook-and-line fishermen. Ranges over all southern waters and throughout the Caribbean.

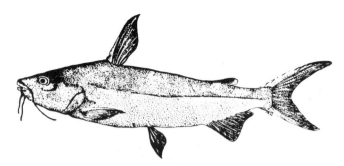

18. HARDHEAD CATFISH   *Arius felis*
Also called Sea Cat.

This pest of the sea picks his food from the leavings of anything. Handle only with a club — they are adept at twisting and will slash barbs into anything in reach.

Catfish comprise one of the largest groups, with over a hundred species, mostly freshwater, but often migrating from fresh- to saltwater. The two shown here are the only marine members in Florida waters. Does the male get his nasty disposition from having to fast for a month while carrying the female's eggs around in his mouth? No loving father, though, he'll devour his offspring once they hatch.

Not prized for food here, but are considered good eating in some countries.

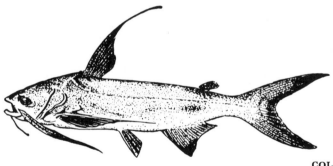

COLOR 48

19. GAFFTOPSAIL CATFISH   *Bagre marinus*
Also called Joe Cat, Whisker Cat.

A good fish which suffers from relationship with his cousin, the Hardhead Cat. A real sport fish that delivers a savage strike and a hard fight, usually caught on lures intended for trout or channel bass in the open Gulf waters. Average weight, 4 lbs.

The bleached skull, shaped roughly like a cross, is often seen in curio shops where it is labeled, "Crucifix Shell."

The pink flesh is pleasantly flavored; skin before cooking.

20. GULF TOADFISH   *Opsanus beta*

Florida's most prolific member of the toadfish family and possibly the ugliest.

All head and appetite, with strong blunt teeth, it will snap like a bulldog at any bait and hangs on. Hides in dock litter, especially old bottles and cans. Often creates a self-imposed prison when it gets into a glass jar and grows too big to ever get out!

21. ATLANTIC MIDSHIPMAN   *Porichthys plectrodon*

Also called Singingfish, Bullhead.

Mud color or bronze with purplish or bluish tinge on top. Paler on sides, yellow belly. A row of luminous photophores arranged in rows on the body like buttons on a uniform prompted the name Midshipman. Average size, 6 inches. Not edible.

Singingfish? Makes a humming sound underwater, using air from the air bladder. Common along Florida's west coast.

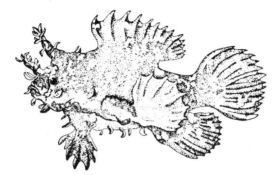

22. SARGASSUMFISH   *Histrio histrio*

A mottled and odd-shaped fish which may have a dozen different colors according to the background of its habitat at that moment. Mostly green and yellow.

A close cousin to the anglerfish, this little fellow lives among the floating beds of seaweed in the tropical waters of America. As the seaweed floats, so goes the fish, and it may wind up almost anywhere there is an ocean current.

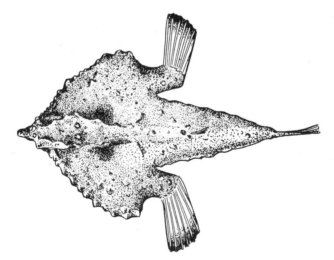

23. SHORTNOSE BATFISH   *Ogcocephalus nasutus*

Brownish-black with mottled warty skin, a big mouth under a button-like nose, and fins that resemble feet.

Grotesque-looking creatures that behave like their ugly relatives, the anglerfish and frogfishes. That is, they have a built-in "fishing rod and bait." A projection from the mouth lures small fish into grabbing distance — where they are immediately gobbled up.

24. PEARL FISH *Carapus bermudensis*

An interesting little fish that lives only inside the sea cucumber and comes out at night to forage. Rarely exceeds 7 inches; averages 3–5 inches.

The flesh is largely transparent, with some pearly or silver-colored patches behind the head. Uses the sharp-pointed tail to gain entry into anal opening of the sea cucumber. If the opening is closed, the fish noses the opening and then, with a whip-like motion, swings its tail past its head and inserts it in the anal opening. When the sea cucumber's sphincter muscle relaxes during respiration, the Pearl Fish slips further in or perhaps all the way in. Instances of three or more fish living inside one sea cucumber have been reported.

25. TROPICAL TWO-WING FLYINGFISH *Exocoetus volitans*

Greenish on back, shading to silver below. Ventral fins white. Average size, 9 inches; largest on record, 18 inches. Food value, poor.

Sometimes travels in large schools in the Atlantic and Gulf waters. Smaller and more round-bodied than their California cousins. They do not actually fly as their name implies; Gliding Fish would be a better name. But they can soar considerable distances when they take off at high speed from the crest of a wave. The "wings" stiffen and the tail vibrates rapidly, creating a "propeller" to help keep them airborne.

26. BALAO   *Hemiramphus balao*

These little fish swim in all warm seas and are valued mostly as bait fish. They bring best results when trolled in the Gulf Stream.

27. ATLANTIC NEEDLEFISH   *Strongylura marina*

Bluish on back, silvery over belly and sides. Average size, 24 inches; largest on record not known.

Although it can't be eaten and is no good for bait, some tourist attractions found a way to make them earn their keep. The sign would say, "Educated Fish." Inside, in an aquarium, the resident Needlefish would leap and cavort on demand — that is, when disturbed.

28. HOUNDFISH   *Tylosurus crocodilus*

Bluish on back, silvery over belly and sides. Average length, 2 feet up to 5 feet.

Has an unusually short and strong beak and solid body. Found in southern waters and as far north as New Jersey. Looks like a giant Needlefish, but is much more dangerous to a small-boat fisherman.

29. ATLANTIC SAURY   *Scomberesox saurus*

Also called Skipper.

Dark on back, silvery on sides and belly.

Travels in large schools. Leaps from water frequently when pursued by larger fish. Spends most of life in open sea, although at times, the schools come close inshore.

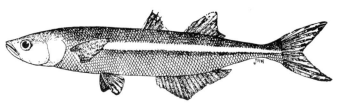

30. INLAND SILVERSIDE   *Menidia beryllina*
Greenish-blue on back, silvery on sides. A carnivorous fish of small size, travels in great schools near the shores of tropical and semi-tropical waters. As a rule is not considered much as food, but is good bait fish.

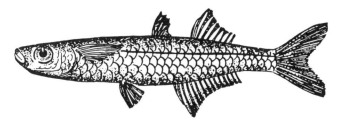

31. ATLANTIC SILVERSIDE   *Menidia menidia*
Waxy, translucent, thickly punctuated with black on top of head; dots on edges of scales. Length, approximately 5 inches.

32. TRUMPETFISH   *Aulostomus maculatus*
Brown to light brown or yellowish. A bony fish, with snout somewhat resembling Pipefish.

Occasionally found in all waters of the Gulf of Mexico. Usually does not exceed 2 feet in length.

33. BLUESPOTTED CORNETFISH   *Fistularia tabacaria*
Color, dark olive on back, pink on belly, with bright blue spots (smaller than a dime) all over body. Normally tropical, has been found as far north as Nova Scotia. Size: may get to 5 or 6 feet.

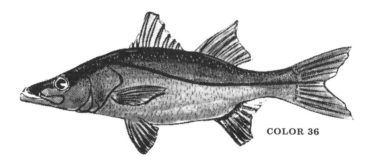

COLOR 41

34. SQUIRRELFISH — *Holocentrus adscensionis*
Also called Red Squirrelfish, Soldierfish.

A pink or reddish fish with large, dark eyes. Inhabiting the offshore reefs of the tropics, they are timid fish by nature, hiding mostly in the daytime and out at night. They spend most of their lives in rocky crevices. Many of the larger fish prey on them for food. Average weight, 1 lb.; occasionally 2 lbs.

Takes a hook readily, especially at night. Comparable to the Red Snapper as a food fish, although the flesh is softer.

COLOR 36

35. SNOOK — *Centropomus undecimalis*
Also called Robalo, Ravillia, Sergeant, Saltwater Pike, Sergeantfish.

Found from Central Florida southward. Can't stand temperatures below 60°:

Olivaceous on back shading into greenish-silver on sides above lateral line, silvery below. A pronounced black lateral line or stripe runs from top of gill cover to center of tail. Once commercial, it may now be taken only by sport fishermen.

This is a saltwater tackle-buster of top rank. Takes to artificial bait with a vim, which endears it to all sportsmen. Prefers anything that moves on top water. Weight, up to 40 lbs. in Florida.

COLOR 37

36. BLACK SEA BASS   *Centropristis striata*

Mottled black, interspersed with lighter colored markings.

Caught mostly on patches of rock surrounded by grass bottom, often in large numbers around wrecks, sometimes as deep as 250 feet. Method of angling is still fishing with lead and hook rigged as for grouper or bottom fish.

Eats barnacles, crabs, small fish, shrimp, or most anything. Any type of cut bait is suitable. No artificial lures are successful when fishing for these fish. Food value: good.

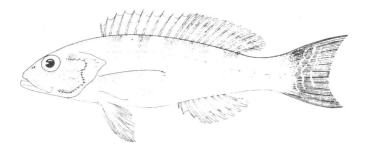

37. SAND PERCH   *Diplectrum formosum*

A prettily colored fish: blue lines on head, blotchy blue horizontal bars, yellow markings on fins. Colors vary with conditions of sandy bottom where they are found. They fan the sand away to make a hole in which to hide. Range from North Carolina to Uruguay. Common in the Gulf of Mexico. Average size, 6-12 inches. Good food value.

THE GROUPERS, which are more often "loners" than "groupers," are sea basses of the family Serranidae, genera *Epinephelus* and *Mycteroperca*. To try to picture or describe coloration, or even markings, is frustrating. Colors change with life stages, depth and clarity of water, or activity — for instance, in the frenzy of feeding. Descriptions therefore are only those "often seen." Also, we have included only those frequently caught in Florida waters. Over 20 species of these two genera, and many more closely related species, occur off our coasts.

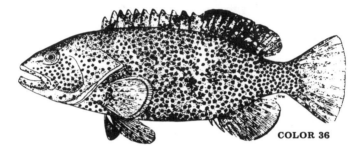

COLOR 36

38. ROCK HIND   *Epinephelus adscensionis*
Reddish-brown cast with olive blotches along sides and back; whitish blotches with pinkish cast over entire body. Head and lower part of body covered with orange spots. This is a valued food fish, commercially important and one of the most beautifully patterned of the groupers. Primarily a reef fish.

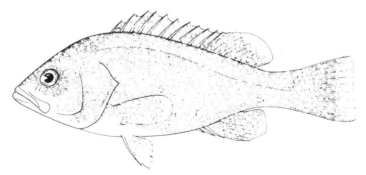

39. SPECKLED HIND   *Epinephelus drummondhayi*
Also called Kitty Mitchell Grouper.
A true grouper, with the shape of a Giant Grouper (Jewfish), yet miniaturized to the size of a large snapper. The coloring is more elaborate than any other grouper. A myriad of brownish, whitish, and pink dots and dashes.

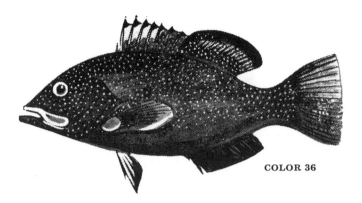

COLOR 36

40. CONEY   *Epinephelus fulvus*

Like all groupers, the Coney has many color phases. Most important identification is the myriad spots covering the entire body
and tail. The fish itself is dark reddish and the spots are yellowish.
It is a fish often confused with the Red Hind. Caught year-round
in southern waters.

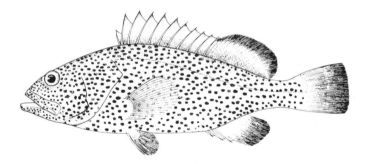

41. RED HIND   *Epinephelus guttatus*

Reddish-brown shading to darker on back and spotted all over
with small scarlet dots. Fins lemon-olive and spotted. Tailfin
margin rather straight with rounded corners. Top of head narrow
between the eyes. These fish are not common on the Florida
coasts; however, they are found in both the Gulf and Atlantic
waters. They are abundant around Cuba, where they are a favorite
food in Havana markets. Usually caught in fairly deep water or on
reefs.

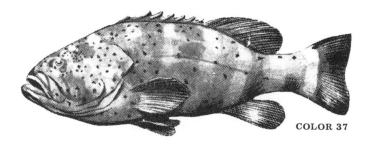

COLOR 37

42. JEWFISH — *Epinephelus itajara*

The giant of the groupers. Averages 20 lbs., often 100 lbs., records to 800 lbs. Brownish body with numerous small dark spots.

The muscle required to get one off the sea bottom is what puts the Jewfish in the game fish class, although they can move fast for a short distance. Prefer deep holes where they seem to sulk and pull straight down when hooked — with shark hooks and chains!

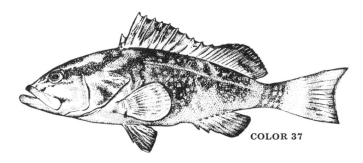

COLOR 37

43. RED GROUPER — *Epinephelus morio*

Olive-grey clouded with pale olive, reddish jaws, salmon cast over body; colors fade when they die.

This is the most common of all fish taken by party boats in the Gulf of Mexico. They bite readily and are caught in great numbers when a school is located. As a food fish, the Red Grouper is a standby, comparable to commercial fish taken anywhere.

Typical bottom fish of the reefs, seldom if ever rising to the surface. Have bladders that are adjusted to depths they inhabit and, when hauled in, these bladders often expand and burst. Offers little resistance when hooked and is not considered a "gamey" fish.

44. WARSAW GROUPER   *Epinephelus nigritus*

Usually caught in deep water. Fights strongly when hooked and darts for a rock hole, trying to stay in its pressure zone. When pulled up, the bladder inflates.

COLOR 36

45. NASSAU GROUPER   *Epinephelus striatus*

Also called White Grouper, Grey Grouper, Rockfish.

The Nassau Grouper is extremely variable in coloration. Ranges from solid white phases to solid greyish-brown. Most often found with four irregular, dark vertical bands on sides, each enclosing small whitish spots. There is a stripe starting at the snout and running through the eye to the base of the dorsal fin. Usually a square jet-black patch is at the root of the tail. All fins are colored like the body, except the dorsal and tail fins, which are bordered with a narrow pale yellow patch.

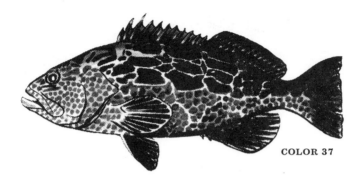

COLOR 37

46. BLACK GROUPER *Mycteroperca bonaci*

There are actually two related forms of the Black Grouper: one found in deep water, and one in shallow water. The deep-water fish is seldom seen and rarely enters the coastal waters of Florida. The shallow-water form is that taken by coastal anglers, mostly in the Florida Keys.

This is the difference — the deep-water fish has small dark patches, close-set; the shallow-water fish has dark splotches which are larger with a squarish shape.

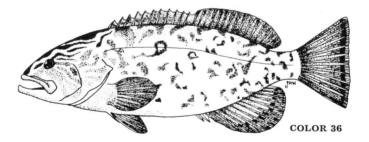

COLOR 36

47. GAG *Mycteroperca microlepis*

Brownish-gray to greenish with blurred dark stripes running back from eye area; dark markings on body often "kiss" shaped. Black bar above upper lip. White-edged tail has blue spots. Fairly common offshore and are excellent food fish. To the dismay of fisheries experts, this fish is usually, and mistakenly, called Black Grouper by Florida west-coast fishermen.

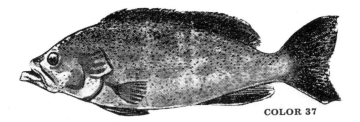

COLOR 37

48. SCAMP — *Mycteroperca phenax*

Light tan with small brown spots over entire body and extending onto fins. If good things come in small packages, the Scamp is an example. Only rarely to 10 lbs., it is considered by many to be the best-eating of the groupers.

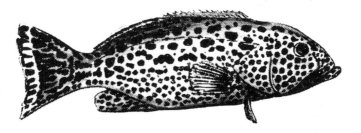

49. YELLOW-FIN GROUPER — *Mycteroperca venenosa*

Also called Rockfish, Bonaci, Spotted Grouper, Princess Rockfish, Black Grouper.

Another color-change artist, it is often confused with several of the other groupers. Body pale green to nearly black, blotches brown. Outer third of pectoral bright yellow. Food value: good.

The brevity of this book precludes showing every grouper that might take your hook in Florida waters. Some others you might encounter are: the Graysby and the Misty Grouper (more likely in the Keys), the Tiger Grouper, the Yellowedge Grouper, the Yellowmouth Grouper and, rarely, the Snowy Grouper (unique in being the only one that is found in both the Atlantic and Pacific). And others!

Of the 400 species that make up the *Serranidae* (sea basses) family, about 60 are found in North America. Over 20 of those belong to the two genera commonly called "groupers." Most of those 20 have been caught in Florida waters. California fishermen are limited to two species. A few groupers range as far north as Massachusetts in summer, but fortunately for us, most of these interesting and succulent fishes make themselves at home in the warm coastal waters of the Gulf and southern Atlantic.

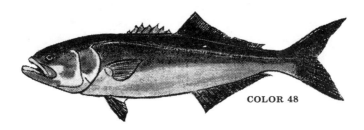

COLOR 48

51. BLUEFISH *Pomatomus saltatrix*
   Also called Blue Snapper, Flatback, Taylor, Greenfish, Skip
Mackerel, Snapping Mackerel.
   True to its name, the Bluefish is a greenish, iridescent blue
shading off to silver at the sides. The pectoral fin is grey-black at the
base. Numerous in winter, but go north for summer. Size is 3 to 10
lbs.
   The Bluefish is the only fish in its family, *Pomitomadae*, which
is probably just as well, for it is the most gluttonous fish in the water,
referred to as a fin-covered chopping machine. A fighter to catch, it
is delicious to eat.

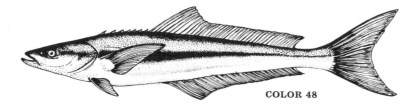

COLOR 48

52. COBIA *Rachycentron canadum*
   Also called Sergeantfish, Oceanic Catfish, Ling, Lemonfish,
Flathead, Cubby-Yew, Crab-Eater, Coalfish, Cavoco, Carbio,
Cabbeo, Black Salmon, Black Bonito.
   A lone-wolf type of fish, usually found around buoys and
channel markers and off-shore wrecks. They will lurk around chan-
nel edges, especially where old rotted pilings offer food for small
fishes. They dart out and strike at the bait when tossed close.

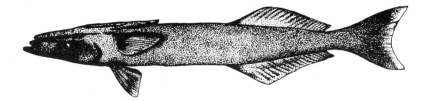

53. REMORA   *Remora remora*
This is the closest thing to a sea-going hitch-hiker. The Remora does not even ask for a ride, but just hitches onto any fish that comes along by clamping on a vacuum cup attachment on the top of his head and riding along. Sizes, up to 12 inches.

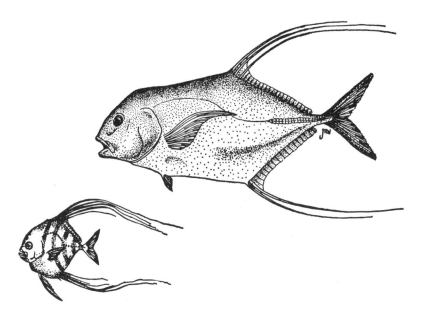

54. AFRICAN POMPANO   *Alectis ciliaris*
Silvery body, bluish-green above. Soft rays of dorsal fins may exceed body length. The very long filiform rays of the young won them the name Threadfish; now considered to be two life-stages of the same fish. Average weight, 2 to 4 lbs., but one specimen weighed in at 42 lbs.

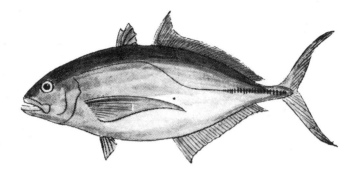

55. YELLOW JACK   *Caranx bartholomaei*

Greenish on back with a broad purple stripe following contour of the fish above lateral line. Long pectoral fin. Found mostly in the Florida Keys, but occasionally caught in all Gulf waters as well as in tropical Atlantic Ocean areas. They strike at trolled baits and put up a lusty fight.

The flesh is strong and is only palatable when smoked or cured in some like manner.

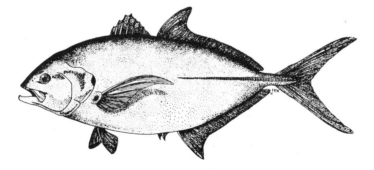

56. BLUE RUNNER   *Caranx crysos*

Also called Hard-Tail Jack, Yellow Jack, Yellow Mackerel, Runner.

Greenish on back and upper sides, shading into a yellowish-silver. Fins almost colorless. Average weight, 16 oz.

Almost always caught trolling, for they feed on live top bait such as sardines and menhaden. At times will attack schools of these fish with such force that the water boils for quite some time as they gorge themselves. Excellent bait for sharks.

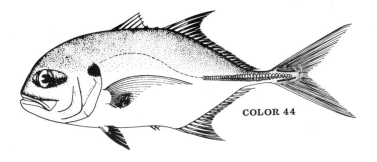

COLOR 44

57. CREVALLE JACK *Caranx hippos*

Also called Cavalla, Horse Crevalle, Skipjack, Toro, Jack, Pompano, Ulua.

Light olive on back, shading to greyish-gold on sides and yellowish on belly. A distinct black spot on gill covers; broad forked tail. Average weight, 2 lbs., but records of 50 lbs. exist.

A savage fighter and rightfully called the bulldog of the sea for the stubborn fight put up when hooked. Some call the Crevalle the strongest and toughest of all fish. They are constantly on the move. Anglers seldom hunt them in particular; they are usually taken when fishing for other fish. They travel in schools and one strike is a signal for all lines to be busy at the same time. A fair-sized Crevalle can put up a 20-minute fight which will leave the fisherman amazed that one fish of the size he has on the line could make such an effort to escape. Edibility only fair.

58. RAINBOW RUNNER *Elegatis bipinnulata*

This is considered to be the rarest of the jacks. They range the grouper-populated reefs in solitary splendor. Only once in a great while is one caught, and then always by trolling. They are very swift. So slim, they seem unrelated to their fatter-bodied relatives. Good game fish and good eating.

59. PILOTFISH *Naucrates ductor*

Looks something like an Amberjack, except for five to six wide vertical dark stripes. Is cylindrical in shape with a blunt nose.

Often found in company of off-shore sharks, giving the appearance of piloting them. Have been observed to range out and discover a bait, then swim back and forth from the shark to the bait as if leading them on.

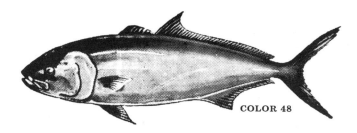

COLOR 48

60. GREATER AMBERJACK *Seriola dumerili*

Also called Cavilia, Horse Crevalle, Skipjack, Toro, Jack, Ulua.

Greenish on back, sides reddish to silvery. The Greater Amberjack has little fear of man and his works, roaming the seas and inspecting fishing boats and coral reefs with equal impartiality. Feeds entirely on live small fish — almost anything from mullet to grunts. An outstanding trait of the Greater Amberjack is curiosity. Whenever one is hooked, the entire school will follow the battling fish to the boat. Another bait presented by fishermen is quickly snapped up, and the entire school can be caught by always having one fish left struggling in the water. It will strike at all kinds of live fish.

A process of smoking this fish has been developed which turns it into a delicious tidbit called Southern Salmon.

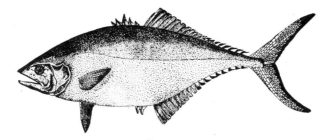

61. LEATHERJACKET   *Oligoplites saurus*

Back is light greenish, sides silvery, leathery skin. Has a small spine which can protrude and give a painful wound.

The small member of the jack family, sometimes used as bait. A very fast swimmer that's exciting to catch in open water. Average size about 12 inches.

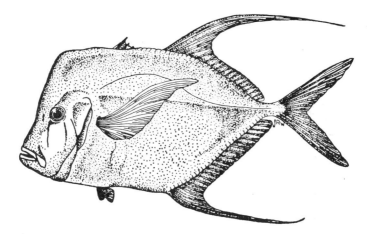

62. LOOKDOWN   *Selene vomer*

Also called Moonfish, Blunt-Nosed Shiner, Jorabado, Old Man of the Sea, Silver Moonfish.

Uniform silvery color. Though often these fish are caught trolling on the Atlantic side, they are rare in Gulf waters. Will strike almost anything they can catch. Average weight, 1 lb., sometimes to 3 lbs.

The flesh is rather oily, as is that of most members of the jack family.

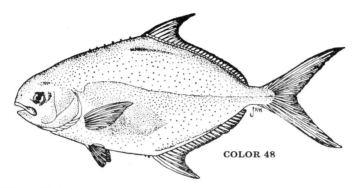

COLOR 48

63. FLORIDA POMPANO
Trachinotus carolinus

Also called Carolina Pompano, Cobbler.

This is the fish that has everything. Epicureans consider it a delight; sport and commercial fishermen seek it with equal fervor. Fun to catch on hook and line with artificial or natural bait; netted by commercial fishermen and now being bred in ponds with some success. Average weight about 1 or 2 lbs., but occasionally to 6 or 7 lbs.

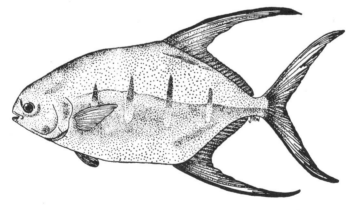

64. PALOMETA
Trachinotus goodei

Bluish over silver; all fins dark.

Feeds on top water minnows and crabs in seaweed. Usually found in deep passes or on edge of inshore reefs. Always on the move. Weight, approximately 3 lbs., usually less.

Easy to distinguish by their long dorsal and anal fin lobes. Often seen in large schools around reefs in shallow to moderate depths. Apparently curious as it will circle skin divers again and again until alarmed.

The four vertical bars distinguish this fish from the Permit, which also exhibits extended dorsal and anal-fin lobes.

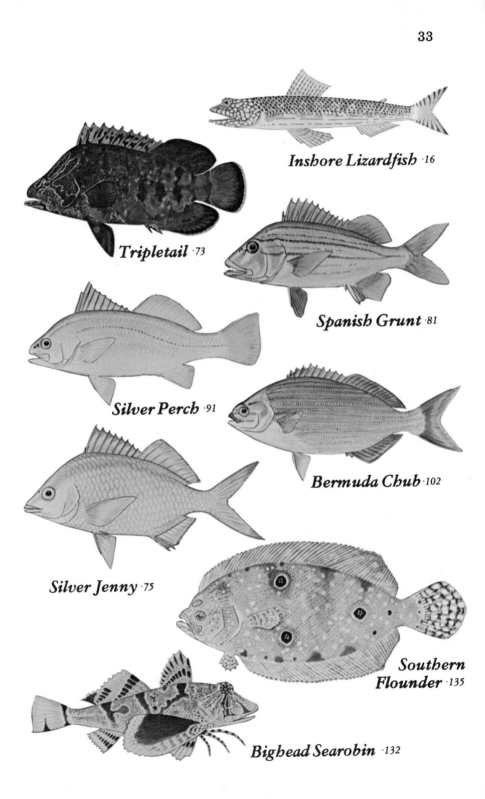

Inshore Lizardfish ·16

Tripletail ·73

Spanish Grunt ·81

Silver Perch ·91

Bermuda Chub ·102

Silver Jenny ·75

Southern Flounder ·135

Bighead Searobin ·132

65. PERMIT
Trachinotus falcatus

Also called Round Pompano, Great Pompano.

Blue on upper sides, top of head darker blue, rest of body silvery with deep golden reflections. Akin to, but much larger than, the Florida Pompano; they are less popular as a food fish.

This fish spooks easily and must be stalked like a deer. Found on shallow flats in the Florida Keys and feeds on sand crabs. The long dorsal fins are first sighted as schools of this fish work across flats where water depth is only 6 inches. A great sport fish. Weight, often up to 25 lbs., occasionally to 50 lbs.

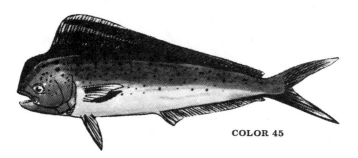

COLOR 45

66. DOLPHIN
Coryphaena hippurus

Also called Dorado, Dourade.

Head of male is higher in the forehead and profile more nearly vertical. Also, males are bluish-gold while females are gold-green, generally. Color description is difficult as their iridescence seems to change suddenly from one hue to another. Once considered inedible, now prized by many as a delicacy. For the fisherman: beautiful, and lightning fast.

67. MUTTON SNAPPER   *Lutjanus analis*

Also called Pargo, Reef King, Muttonfish.

Black, orange-red to salmon colored. Has black spot on either side of back near juncture of hard and soft dorsal. Prominent, narrow blue streak from nostril to eye.

They are caught still fishing over the reefs with cut bait, much the same as grouper and grunts. A popular fishing method is to drift over likely spots. The Mutton Snapper will dart out and snatch a bait which passes close to him.

Next to the Red Snapper, this is the largest of the snapper family. Good food fish. Weight, sometimes to 30 lbs.

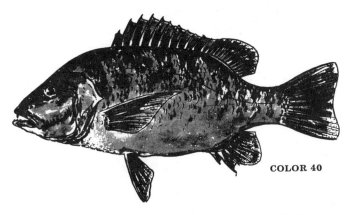

COLOR 40

68. SCHOOLMASTER   *Lutjanus apodus*

Also called Sea Lawyer, Black Snapper, Caji.

Reddish-brown on back, shading into an orange cast on sides. Reddish tint and deeper orange below. Broad greenish-white vertical bars from back to lower part of sides. Abundant on reefs and bottoms where grouper and grunts are found.

One of the most beautiful of the snappers. Has rather large scales and a very large canine tooth on either side of upper jaw. Edibility: very good.

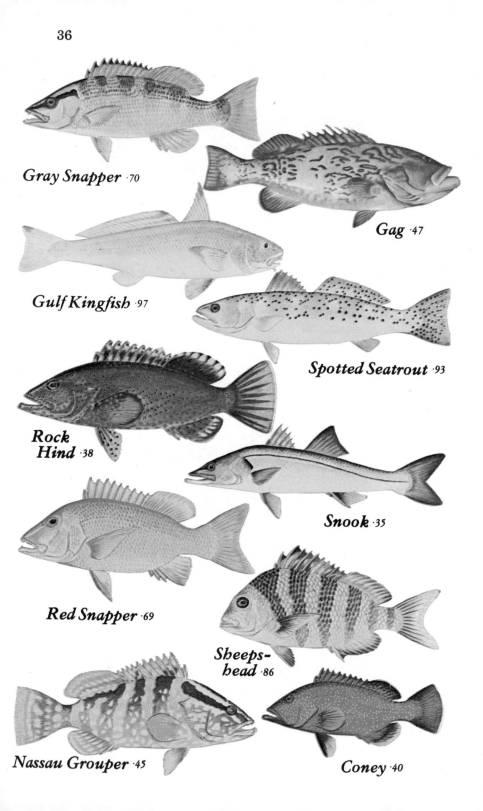

Gray Snapper ·70

Gag ·47

Gulf Kingfish ·97

Spotted Seatrout ·93

Rock Hind ·38

Snook ·35

Red Snapper ·69

Sheeps-head ·86

Nassau Grouper ·45

Coney ·40

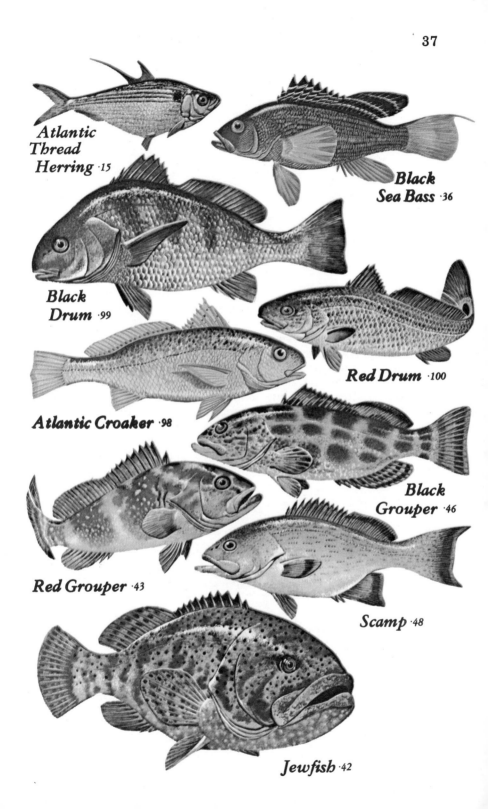

Atlantic
Thread
Herring ·15

Black
Sea Bass ·36

Black
Drum ·99

Red Drum ·100

Atlantic Croaker ·98

Black
Grouper ·46

Red Grouper ·43

Scamp ·48

Jewfish ·42

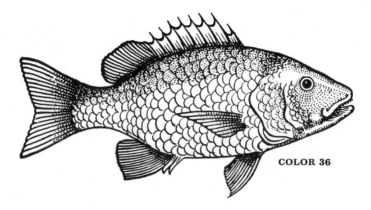

COLOR 36

69. RED SNAPPER
Lutjanus campechanus

Also called Acara, Aya, Pensacola Snapper, Pensacola Red Snapper, Pargo Colorado.

Deep brick-red all over, except shading to a paler red on belly and throat. Fins and eyes are red.

This is a deep-water fish, taken mostly by commercial fishermen in waters of the Atlantic and Gulf. Seldom caught on anything but a stout hand line. Some of the best snapper bottom is 200 to 300 feet deep. When a school is located, they usually bite fast and the catch is heavy. Food value: superb.

Natural food is small fish, crabs, and shrimp. Cut mullet is excellent bait. Rock bottom is best Red Snapper fishing. Range is from the Florida coast to the West Indies and Brazil.

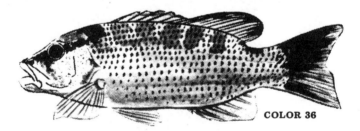

COLOR 36

70. GRAY SNAPPER
Lutjanus griseus

Also called Mangrove Snapper, Black Snapper.

Bronze-green above, shading into brassy-red on sides and light grey on belly, interspersed with darker markings on scales. Sure to be recognized by the dark streak which runs from nose across eye and fades toward dorsal fin. Looks like a bluish-black slash. This is the wisest and most alert member of the snappers. While quite numerous in bays and bayous, especially around mangrove-studded islands, they are not easily caught.

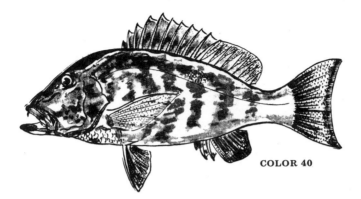

COLOR 40

71. LANE SNAPPER   *Lutjanus synagris*

Also called Spot Snapper, Red-Tail Snapper, Biajaiba, Silk Snapper, Candy Snapper.

Rose colored, shading off to silvery with an olive cast. Series of deep golden stripes along sides. One of the smallest members of the snapper family.

This beautifully colored fish is abundant in shallow water, in company with grunts and similar shore fishes. Usually a solitary fish, not often in schools. Frequently found around wharves and river mouths and inlets.

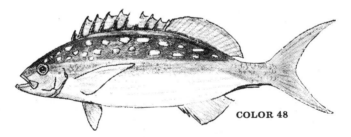

COLOR 48

72. YELLOWTAIL SNAPPER   *Ocyurus chrysurus*

Also called Yellowtail, Rabirubia.

Variable coloring. Usual color, greyish-blue with yellow spots and lines. A broad yellow stripe from snout to tail. Lower parts of body rosy. Fins yellow. Has deeply forked tail. Top of head has no scales. Average weight, 1 lb., occasionally to 6 lbs.

Very abundant in Florida in channels and among the Keys. Usually found in medium depths in inlets and lagoons. Feeds day and night on smaller fishes, crabs, and shrimp.

Will take most any bait offered which looks as if it is alive. Put up a good fight for their size.

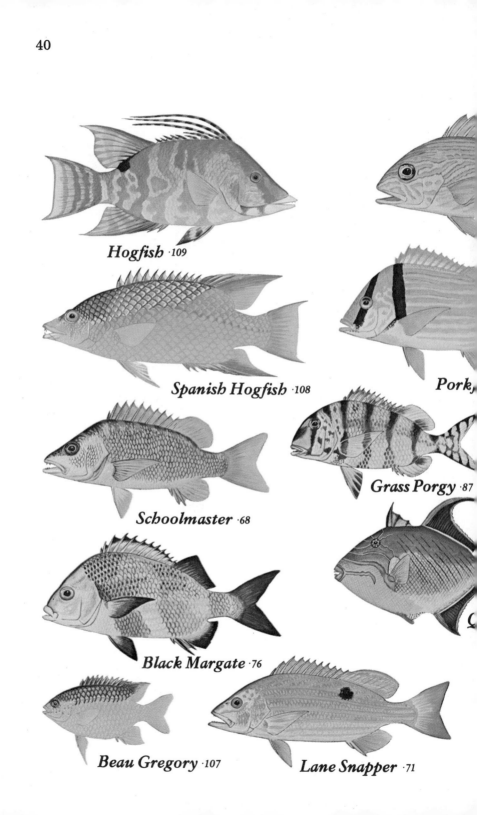

Hogfish ·109

Spanish Hogfish ·108

Pork

Schoolmaster ·68

Grass Porgy ·87

Black Margate ·76

Beau Gregory ·107

Lane Snapper ·71

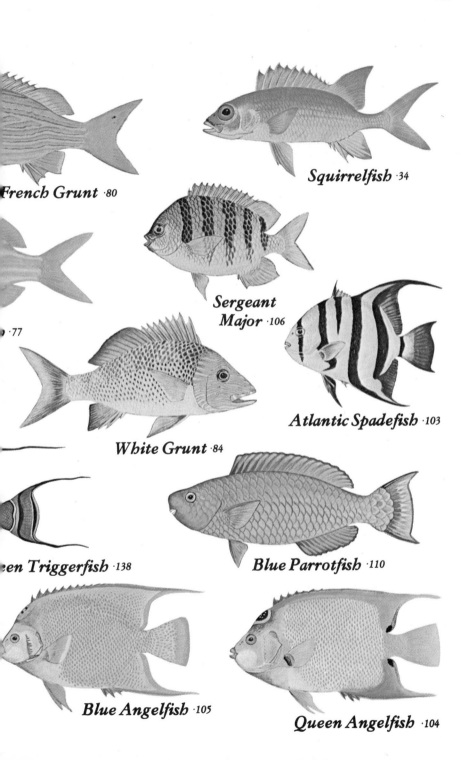

French Grunt ·80

Squirrelfish ·34

Sergeant Major ·106

·77

Atlantic Spadefish ·103

White Grunt ·84

en Triggerfish ·138

Blue Parrotfish ·110

Blue Angelfish ·105

Queen Angelfish ·104

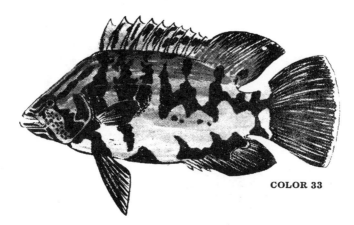

COLOR 33

73. TRIPLETAIL — *Lobotes surinamensis*

Dull black, silvery-grey sides and belly. Young have greyish or yellow irregular spots. Generally an open-water fish, they sometimes swim around wrecks and buoys (winning them the name "Snag Drifters").

Caught mostly still fishing, rarely taking a trolled lure. Readily takes a hook baited with shrimp, crabs, and such. Good eating, but bony. Weight, up to 20 lbs.

Wide range: Massachusetts to Uruguay, Africa, Mediterranean, and southern Europe.

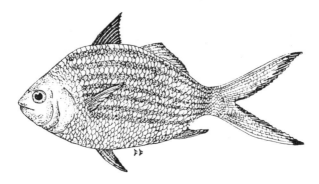

74. STRIPED MOJARRA — *Diapterus plumieri*

Also called Sand Perch, Goat, Sand Brim.

Easily recognized by their deeply forked tails. Average weight, 10 oz. up to 2 lbs. Size, known to reach 1 foot in length, but averages 4 to 8 inches. Food value: good, but a bit on the boney side.

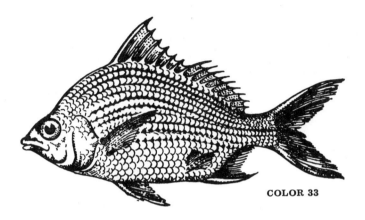

COLOR 33

75. SILVER JENNY   *Eucinostomus gula*

Coloring of grey beginning at dorsal fin, gradually brightening to silver over rest of body, growing very light around belly. Elevated back, pointed snout. Average size, 6 inches.

Very gregarious and found chiefly in brackish tidal waters and shallow sandy beaches. Good bait fish for Snook and Tarpon.

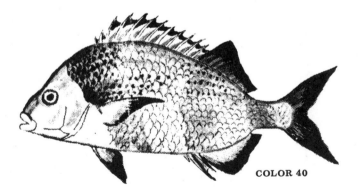

COLOR 40

76. BLACK MARGATE   *Anisotremus surinamensis*

Also called White Margate, Pompon.

Colors subject to rapid change. Has heavy large scales, large eyes and dark markings on body and fins. General color is silvery. Margate fish is usually very light, almost pearl-grey. Dark spots on scales form wide-spaced longitudinal lines, most distinct on upper sides.

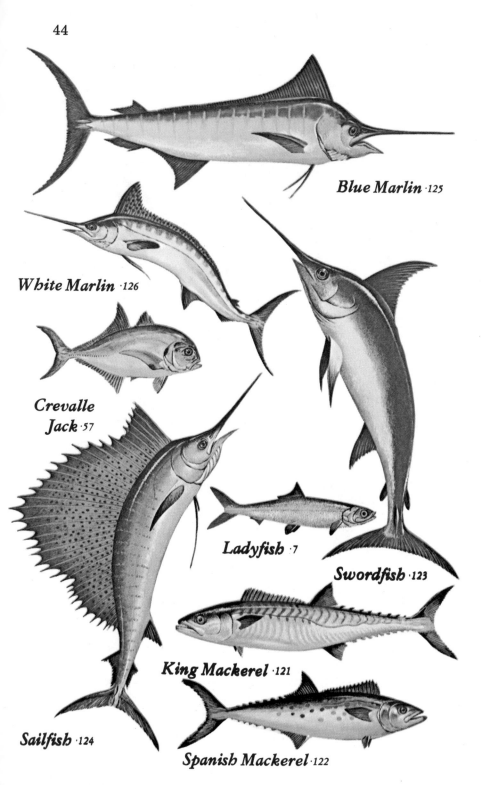

Blue Marlin ·125

White Marlin ·126

Crevalle Jack ·57

Ladyfish ·7

Swordfish ·123

King Mackerel ·121

Sailfish ·124

Spanish Mackerel ·122

Albacore ·120

Tarpon ·8

Atlantic Bonita ·119

Dolphin ·66

Great Barracuda ·113

Wahoo ·117

Bonefish ·9

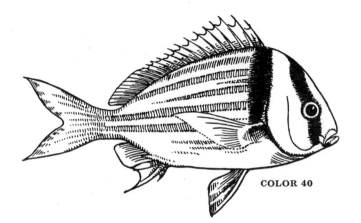

COLOR 40

77. PORKFISH   *Anisotremus virginicus*

These fish always run in small schools and are fast strikers when bait is cast among them. They are the prey of many larger fish and elude their enemies by darting in and out of coral rocks. Most always found where coral and rock bottom is honeycombed with caves and holes. They belong to a fast-swimming group, mostly traveling together in unison as they swim.

Size: up to 12 or 14 inches. Food value: good.

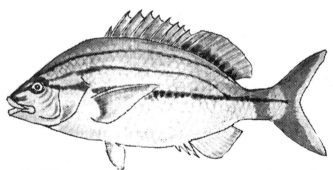

78. MARGATE   *Haemulon album*

Also called Margaret Grunt, Marketfish, Redmouth Grunt.

Usually a light pearl-grey, has longitudinal lines most distinct on upper sides. Fish may turn greenish when caught. Lips yellowish. Younger specimens lack stripes.

Usually a deep-water fish, except when feeding. They like to pick up sea fleas and small crabs from bottom. Are caught in large enough quantities for market, although not as good a food as grouper. Do not keep too well.

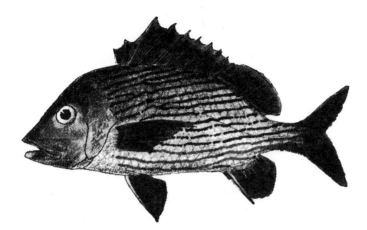

79. BLACK GRUNT *Haemulon bonariense*

Also called Hoarse Muffle, Snorer, Blower, Corocoro.

Brownish above, fading to lighter below. Has typical grunt mouth and big eye. One long spine on leading edge of anal fin. Usually 11 to 12 spines in dorsal. Spine section higher than rayed section, which is rounded on top. Fins light, tail black.

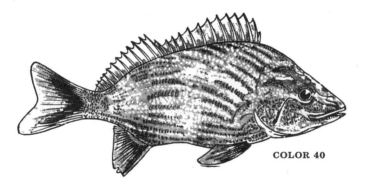

COLOR 40

80. FRENCH GRUNT *Haemulon flavolineatum*

Also called Yellowstriped Grunt, Open-Mouthed Grunt, Ronco Contenado.

Ground color grey-blue. Longitudinal yellow or brassy stripes above the lateral line. One stripe crosses the others running from the head to end of dorsal base. Fins bright yellow. Weight, usually less than 1 lb.

Feed chiefly at night on small spineless fish. A choice meal for all game fish, they spend most of their lives hiding out. Will grab at a baited hook, especially if it has a piece of clam or oyster as bait.

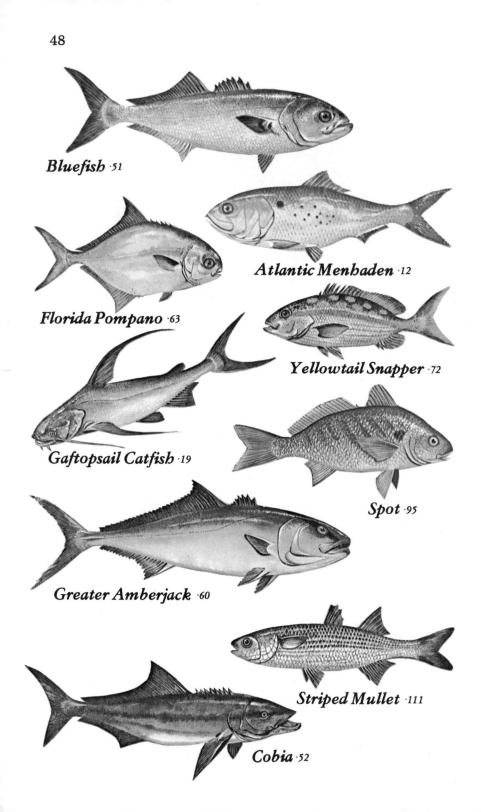

Bluefish ·51

Atlantic Menhaden ·12

Florida Pompano ·63

Yellowtail Snapper ·72

Gaftopsail Catfish ·19

Spot ·95

Greater Amberjack ·60

Striped Mullet ·111

Cobia ·52

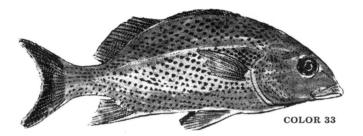

COLOR 33

81. SPANISH GRUNT — *Haemulon macrostomum*

Also called Ronco Blanco, Corocoro, Brown Grunt, Ronco.

Grey with iridescence or shading. Scales have small brown spots which form wavy streaks below the lateral line. Black spot on gill cover. Mouth lining bright red.

They live in fairly shallow water around reef bottoms. Found both in schools and singly. School mostly in summer — their spawning time. Quite often taken around channel inlets. Average weight, 1 lb.

82. COTTONWICK — *Haemulon melanurum*

Also called West Indies Grunt, Comical Grunt, Caesar Grunt.

Eyes an unusual shade of bright glossy blue. Ground color on sides dark olive, almost black. Lateral line running from just above the mouth to tail is most prominent. Belly golden yellow. Mottled with silver at lower jaw and nose and about the anal fin. Tail is golden yellow, slightly edged with black. Native of West Indies. Size: to 1 foot. Food value: fair.

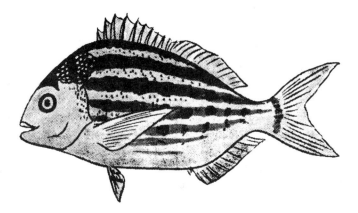

83. SAILOR'S CHOICE   *Haemulon parra*
Also called Ronco, Bastard Grunt.

Silver with brown markings. Inside of mouth red. Black spot under opercular edge.

Common panfish of the grunt family, caught in most all inshore Gulf and Atlantic fishing spots. Good food fish.

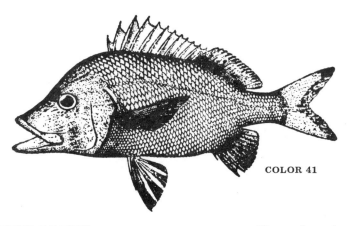

COLOR 41

84. WHITE GRUNT   *Haemulon plumieri*
Also called Black Grunt, Boat Grunt, Boca Colorado, Cachicate, Ronco, Ronco Grande, Squirrelfish, Key West Grunt, Flannel-Mouth Grunt.

The White Grunt is the most plentiful and important of the family. Silvery-white body, top of head yellow or bronze. Characteristic of all the grunts is a red mouth (inside) and their "kissing" behavior. The name derives from the muffled grunting sounds they make under water. Edibility: good.

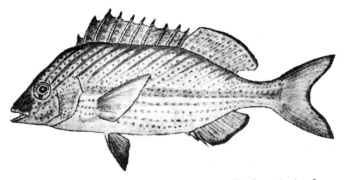

85. PIGFISH
Orthopristis chrysoptera

Also called Piggie.

Usually light blue and silver-striped nose, with brown spots on snout. Has a blue streak on side of upper lip. Mouth whitish inside. Dorsal fin spotted with bronze; tail yellow, dusky tipped.

A hardy fish and, in ordinary conditions, one of the most plentiful of panfish on the shores of the Gulf of Mexico. Not only highly versatile in fish recipes, it is also the finest tarpon bait.

COLOR 36

86. SHEEPSHEAD
Archosargus probatocephalus

Also called Convict Fish, Sardo Raiado.

A deep compressed body with 12 or 13 black and white alternating vertical stripes along sides from top to bottom.

The Sheephead gets its name from the resemblance of its teeth to that of sheep. The powerful jaws and strong teeth are used to clip the bait in quick bites which make it a difficult fish to hook. Probably one of the best known of the sport fishes caught along coastal fishing grounds and around pilings where they use their incisor-like teeth to pick off shellfish and barnacles. Average weight, 2 to 3 lbs, sometimes to 20 lbs. or more. Food value, good.

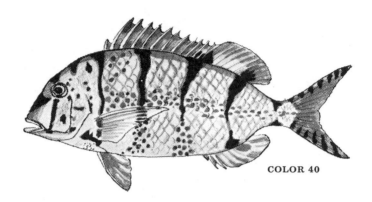

COLOR 40

87. GRASS PORGY   *Calamus arctifrons*

Has a band from forepart of cheek to the tail; cheek is bright yellow; fins are marked with black. Feeds mostly on small mollusks, very fond of shrimp. Fights determinedly for a short time, then gives up. Found on grass banks. Native from Cape Hatteras throughout the South Atlantic and the Gulf of Mexico. A small fish, rarely reaching 12 inches in size. Good eating.

88. LITTLEHEAD PORGY   *Calamus proridens*

Silvery, with bright reflections above, much brighter than other species. Each scale above middle of side has a spot of blue at base. These form longitudinal streaks. Spots on lower part of body pale orange. Average weight, ½ lb., largest on record, 3 lbs. Food value, good.

Mostly found in Florida Keys, moderately common in Gulf.

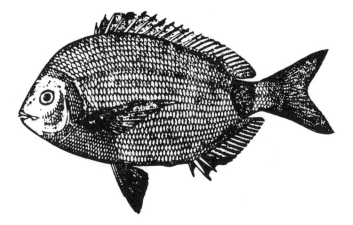

89. SPOTTAIL PINFISH *Diplodus holbrooki*

Also called Spot-Tail Porgy, Pinfish, Spot.

Somewhat resembling the common pinfish, yet has a deeper body and firmer flesh. Food value: better eating than the pinfish.

A small fish that reaches only 8 inches in length. Found along our South Atlantic and Gulf coasts from Cape Hatteras to Cedar Key. Around Lake Worth it is called a "Jimmy." Considered an excellent panfish.

90. PINFISH *Lagodon rhomboides*

Also called Shiner, Sailors Choice, Bream, Choby, Chopa Sina, Porgy, Scup, Spanish Porgy.

Has distinctive black spot behind gill cover. A common fish found in quantities in all southern waters around grassy flats and about docks. Used extensively as bait fish for tarpon and grouper fishing. Size: to 14 inches. Food value: good.

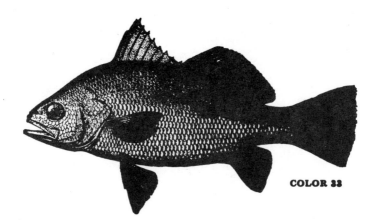

COLOR 33

91. SILVER PERCH   *Bairdiella chrysoura*

A silvery little panfish with a slight shading of blue above a white belly. Size: small; Weight: 8 to 16 oz.

One of the most abundant of panfish in the bays bordering on the Gulf of Mexico shores. They are the joy of Midwestern visitors to Florida, who catch them by the bucketful. Most always referred to as "Butterfish."

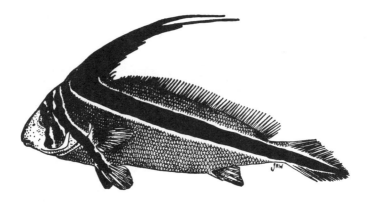

92. JACKKNIFE-FISH   *Equetus lanceolatus*

A rarity among the drum tribe in western Gulf waters, but seen more often around the Florida Keys. The stripe is black. Unmistakeable in shape and coloring for identity. The striking appearance of this fish, seen occasionally from the bridges and causeways of the Florida Keys Overseas Highway, is an important tourist attraction. They are also featured residents of aquariums in Florida cities.

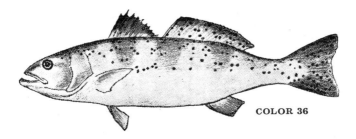

COLOR 36

93. SPOTTED SEATROUT   *Cynoscion nebulosus*

Also called Spotted Squeteague, Speckled Trout and, erroneously, Weakfish.

There is often confusion in the identity of the two fish shown on this page. Both are members of the weakfish clan, having the same soft flesh and easily-torn mouth. Both are spotted, but the Seatrout has larger spots and they extend onto the fins and tail.

Mainstay of all southern coastal fishing, it is important both as a sport and commercial catch. Excellent fish for the table, lean and easily scaled and filleted.

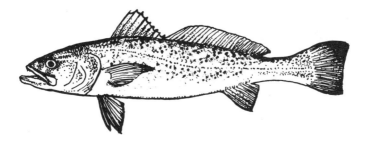

94. WEAKFISH   *Cynoscion regalis*

Also called Squeteague, Summer Trout, Saltwater Trout.

The general shape of the two fish on this page is much the same. Differences to note: the spots of the Weakfish are small and do not extend onto the fins and tail. However, the scales of the Weakfish extend onto the fins, but do not on the Seatrout.

Like the Seatrout, this fish is good food, but should be eaten soon after being caught.

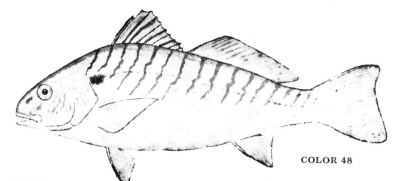

COLOR 48

95. SPOT   *Leiostomus xanthurus*

Also called Lafayette, Flat Croaker.

Brownish-silver color with a head like a croaker and a spot just behind the gill edge; has light diagonal wavy stripes. Edible.

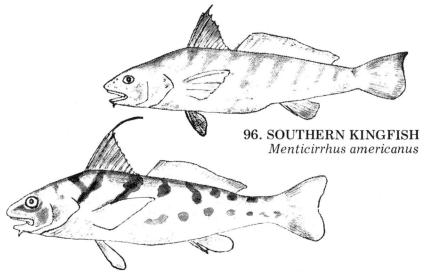

96. SOUTHERN KINGFISH
Menticirrhus americanus

97. NORTHERN KINGFISH   *Menticirrhus saxatilis*

The old name "Whiting" may have been a better choice since "Kingfish" probably means King Mackerel to most fishermen. The Southern Kingfish goes by a long list of aliases. It has distinct dark blotches running obliquely down and forward. Markings on the Northern Kingfish are more irregular, with one at the nape forming a V with the adjacent bar; has a long dorsal spine. A third member, the Gulf Kingfish, *M. littoralis* (page 36) is silvery grey, lacking both marking and elongated pectoral fin. Range of the three overlap, but the Southern King is most dominant in Florida waters. All good to eat.

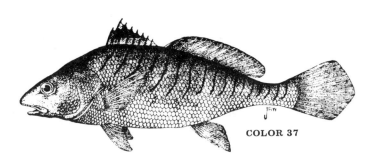

COLOR 37

98. ATLANTIC CROAKER   *Micropogonias undulatus*
Also called Chut, Grunter, Corvina, Crocus, Rocodina.

Brassy above, lighter below, middle part of body has short irregular, dusky, vertical bars crossing the lateral line. Many dark brown spots on the side of back, irregularly placed.

COLOR 37

99. BLACK DRUM   *Pogonias cromis*
Color varies with habitat. Those in the bays are dusky or bronze with indistinct stripes; in the Gulf, are silvery with very dark bands. Several large barbels on underside of jaw. Grow quite large — sometimes over 100 lbs. Smaller ones edible, but not prized as food.

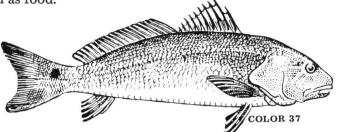

COLOR 37

100. RED DRUM   *Sciaenops ocellatus*
Also called Redfish, Bar Bass, Reef Bass, Saltwater Bass, Red Bass, Sea Bass, Channel Bass, Red Horse.

Greyish, irridescent sides which shade to a copperish-red toward the back. As the fish grows larger, it becomes red all over. One or more black spots at base of tail. Good food fish.

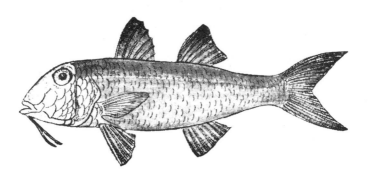

101. RED GOATFISH *Mullus auratus*

Also called Surmullet, Red Mullet.

Scarlet color with two distinct yellow bands. Sides of head silvery. Found on snapper banks of Gulf of Mexico. Not abundant, but good food fish. The Spotted Goatfish, with 3 dark spots, also occurs in the same range. Both edible.

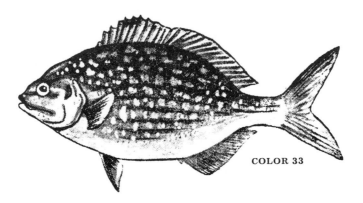

COLOR 33

102. BERMUDA CHUB *Kyphosus sectatrix*

Also called Rudderfish, Chopa.

Color varies, but generally dark, checkered with faint stripes of white or yellow to grey. A great bait-stealer. Successful fishermen land it with small hooks because its mouth is so small.

Plentiful, especially in the Atlantic. Good eating, but the sooner cooked after catching, the better.

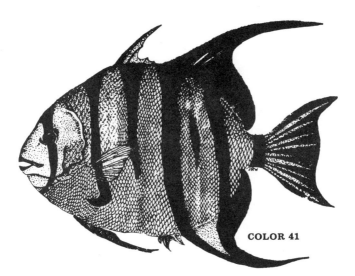

COLOR 41

103. ATLANTIC SPADEFISH   *Chaetodipterus faber*
Prominently marked by vertical bars of black and silver. As the fish grows older, the markings fade. An abundant fish in certain localities about piers and bridges. Always nibbling at the barnacles and along shell-encrusted seawalls. Expert bait-stealers. Weight: averages 2 to 3 lbs. Food value: considered gourmet fare by some.

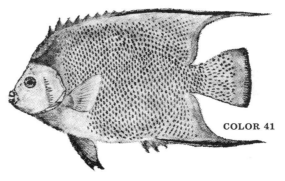

COLOR 41

104. QUEEN ANGELFISH   *Holacanthus ciliaris*
One of the most beautiful of marine fishes. Yellowish body with generous dab of blue at base of head. Primarily a West Indian species, reaching Florida in the Keys where it is sometimes called Yellow Angel.

105. BLUE ANGELFISH (page 41)   *Holacanthus bermudensis*
Most common, ranging from the Bahamas to Brazil. Juveniles are striped. Brilliant as they are, they can appear inconspicuous in their natural colorful habitat of coral reefs.

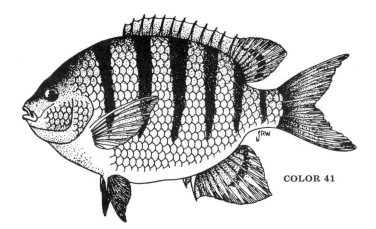

COLOR 41

106. SERGEANT MAJOR   *Abudefduf saxatilis*

Stripes are bright yellow and black. An abundant species of small fish which gathers in swarms around docks, pilings, and tide rips on coral or rock bottoms. They can change color if necessary to accommodate themselves to surroundings. Size: averages 6 inches. Food value: edible.

Spend their time nibbling barnacles from pilings, etc. Although quite small on the whole, they make an excellent little panfish. Can be caught with a small hook and a bit of oyster for bait.

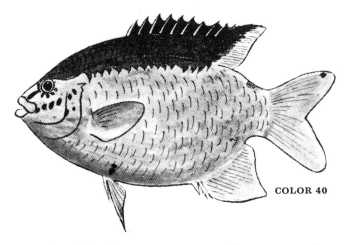

COLOR 40

107. BEAUGREGORY   *Pomacentrus leucostictus*

Yellow on belly and blue on back; large scales. An aggressive little fish of the tropics. Usually appropriate any large empty shell for nests and will defend themselves against attacks of any size enemy. Fine aquarium fish.

COLOR 40

108. SPANISH HOGFISH   *Bodianus rufus*
These handsomely colored reef fish are members of the wrasse family, which are mostly inedible; however, hogfishes are acceptable food fish. Size. to 2 feet.

109. HOGFISH (page 40)   *Lachnolaimus maximus*
Bright colors changing frequently to match background. Characterized by elongated snout and three streamer-like dorsal spines. Feeds on mollusks and shellfish. Takes bait (especially shrimp) on still fishing line.

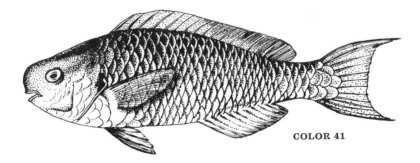

COLOR 41

110. BLUE PARROTFISH   *Scarus coeruleus*
This is one of the larger parrotfishes, believed to attain lengths of 3 feet. Can be identified by fleshy lump on forehead which increases in size with age. Native to West Indies, but has been seen occasionally as far north as the Chesapeake Bay. Several other parrotfishes live in Florida and Caribbean waters.

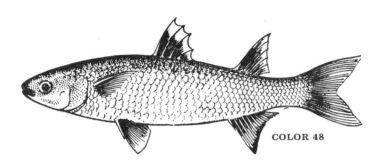

COLOR 48

111. STRIPED MULLET   *Mugil cephalus*

There are about a 100 species of mullet throughout the world, along every tropical or temperate coastline. Nowhere are they more abundant than in Florida, where in pioneer days, the water literally swarmed with them. They are vegetarians, eat grasses exclusively, and have a gizzard comparable to that of a chicken. Long a leading commercial fish, it has always been food on the table to anyone willing to throw a cast net. Known to range far inland where, in muddy rivers, they are considered less palatable than those taken from Florida clearer waters.

Mullet is rather oily, which has given it the unsavory sounding name Fatback. Great as smoked fish and good pan-fried; the roe may not be caviar, but many people prize it.

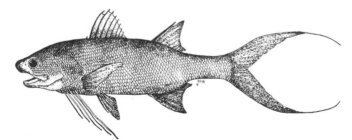

112. ATLANTIC THREADFIN   *Polydactylus octonemus*

Light olivaceous, belly whitish, pectoral black in adult.

A family of tropical fishes inhabiting, in large part, the waters of the Atlantic and Gulf coasts; elsewhere, they are rare. Usually found on sandy bottoms and in shallow water. Take a hook fairly easily when baited with cut mullet or crabs. Size: averages 12 inches.

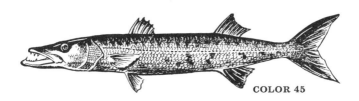

COLOR 45

113. GREAT BARRACUDA   *Sphyraena barracuda*

Also called Sea Tiger, 'Cuda, Saltwater Pike, Picuda, Muskellunge, Sea Pike.

Dark grey on back, sometimes appearing smokey-black. Pronounced spots on sides which turn silvery below lateral line. Has very long sharp teeth, slightly hooked inward. Built like a torpedo, and very swift to start, but does not run great distances on one impulse. A savage fish that will often slash at objects more from meanness or curiosity than from hunger.

114. BANDED JAWFISH   *Opistognathus macrognathus*

Maroon with white spots. Has very large mouth; eyes bulge like a frogfish's; dorsal fin runs entire length of body and is flexible. Snaps continuously when out of water. Has toadfish characteristic of opening mouth wide, but does not bite. Size: small (6 inches or less).

115. SOUTHERN STARGAZER   *Astroscopus y-graecum*

Brownish on back with many spots, like polka-dot design. Small beady eyes, large pectoral fins. Turned-up mouth, with eyes on top of head.

A fish of shallow water, caught in the Gulf of Mexico, but probably also a fish of colder climes. Has power to give electric shock with plates in top of head. Not much known about this species.

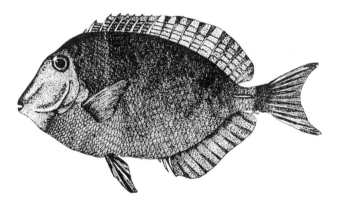

116. DOCTORFISH   *Acanthurus chirurgus*

Also called Surgeonfish, Lancetfish, Medicos, Barberos (Barberos is Spanish for barber — the first practitioners of surgery).

They carry a "razor" — a sharp spine on each side of tail. Body brownish-grey with bluish fins. Weight: averages ½ lb.

Like the mullet, these fish are herbivorous and have gizzard-like stomachs. Food value: poor.

COLOR 45

117. WAHOO
Acanthocybium solandri

Also called Ocean Barracuda, Pacific Kingfish, Peto, Guahu, Queenfish, Guarapucu.

Upper sides dark greenish or steel-blue shading to paler silver. Fins dark. Grey or yellowish bands run down from the back. These are more distinct in the young.

Termed the fastest fish that swims. The first sizzling run of this powerful speedster defies all-star drag reels or human exertion. Weight: averages 15 to 20 lbs., but sometimes to 150 lbs. Edible.

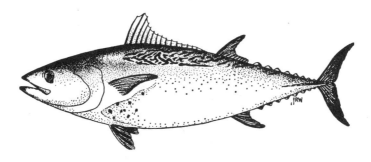

118. LITTLE TUNNY
Euthynnus alletteratus

Also called Little Tuna, Blue Bonita, False Albacore.

Bluish above with silver belly. Several oblique, wavy lines above the lateral line; black irregular blotches below the pectoral fin. Although they range from New England to Brazil, they are most often sought in Florida waters in summer and fall when schools of them appear close to shore and in the bays. Average around 6 or 8 lbs., but some 30-pounders are brought in. A good game fish, but gets low marks in the food-value department.

COLOR 45

119. ATLANTIC BONITO   *Sarda sarda*

Also called Boston Mackerel, Frigate Mackerel, African Bonito, Little Tunny, Bone-eater, Bloater, Bonejack, Skipjack.

Bluish-steel above shading off to silvery sides which become white on belly. Dark stripes run obliquely down and forward from back to lateral line. Weight: 4 to 15 lbs.

Fun to catch; they're fighters — but not very good for eating.

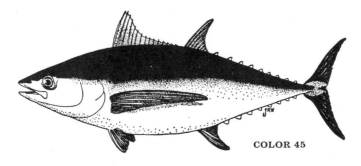

COLOR 45

120. ALBACORE   *Thunnus alalunga*

Also called Long-Finned Albacore, Long-Finned Tuna, Abrego, Alilonghi, German.

Dark blue on top shading to light blue below. Belly silvery-white. Has unusually long pectoral fins which are nearly half as long as the fish. More common in the Pacific than in the Atlantic waters. This is the fish you buy in cans as tuna. Weight: averages 10 to 20 lbs.

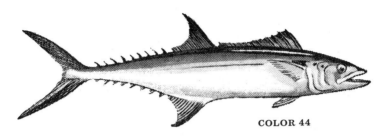

COLOR 44

121. KING MACKEREL — *Scomberomorus cavalla*

Also called Kingfish, Cero, Cavalla, Sierra.

Dark on back, shading to silvery sides and white belly. The great King Mackerel is a migratory fish which travels through the Gulf waters in spring and fall, providing anglers with several weeks of unexcelled fishing. The King Mackerels usually appear off the Florida coasts around March and again in October or November. The schools are large and fishing gets exciting; boats working the schools present a state of grand confusion as bow-to-stern fishermen battle with many fish hooked at the same time. Size, 8 to 20 lbs. Edibility, poor to good, depending on your recipe.

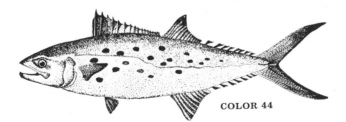

COLOR 44

122. SPANISH MACKEREL — *Scomberomorus maculatus*

Also called Spotted Speedster.

Dark bluish-brown on back with golden spots both above and below the lateral line. Silvery on belly. Staple food fish of southern waters. Often taken by netting, but can be caught with rod and reel. Average size, 2 lbs. or less.

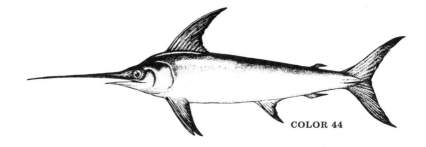

COLOR 44

123. SWORDFISH   *Xiphias gladius*
Also called Broadbill.

Occurs on both sides of the Atlantic and in the Pacific, but more frequently along the eastern coast from Nova Scotia to Cuba. Makes powerful runs, often leaping from the water. Tender mouths tear easily when hooked. Commercial fishermen harpoon them; some captured in this manner weighed over 1200 lbs. Largest rod and reel record, 1182 lbs. Edibility judged to be excellent by diners ordering swordfish steaks in restaurants everywhere.

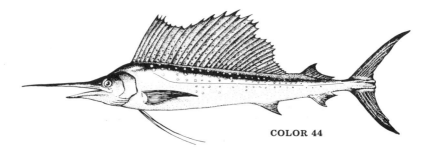

COLOR 44

124. SAILFISH   *Istiophorus platypterus*
Also called Pez Vela, Spearfish, Spikefish.

Purple, overlaying a bright blue, with green stripe shading into paler green sides. It is now generally agreed that Atlantic and Pacific sailfish are the same; they have been thought to be different species. The Atlantic specimens average 20 to 50 lbs., up to 125 lbs. Their Pacific counterparts are much larger. Edibility: excellent.

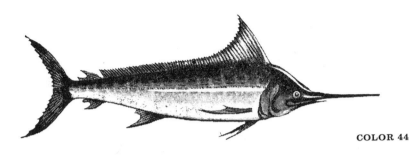

COLOR 44

125. BLUE MARLIN — *Makaira nigricans*

Occurs in both Atlantic and Pacific. Dorsal fin higher and more pointed than that of the White Marlin. Average weight, 100 lbs., but may reach 1500 lbs. Like other billfishes, it is the females that reach great size, and apparently grow larger in the Pacific. Brilliant cobalt back with silvery sides and belly. Vertical bars on the sides disappear when fish dies. Edibility: good.

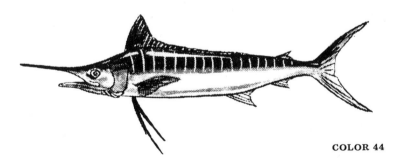

COLOR 44

126. WHITE MARLIN — *Tetrapturus albidus*

Occurs all over the Atlantic. The smallest of the marlins, rarely reaching 150 lbs. Generally lighter in color and leans more toward green than blue. The Striped Marlin, *T. audar*, is thought by many to be most audacious fighter, but no marlin is a piker in that area, and the White's acrobatics surely put it in the big game class.

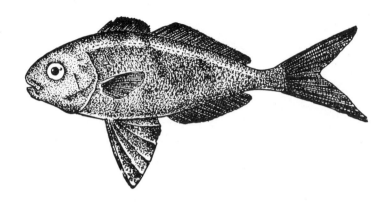

127. MAN-OF-WAR FISH
Nomeus gronovii

Companion of the Portuguese Man-of-War, the stinging jelly-fish that drifts on tropical waters. Lurks among the tentacles to feast on the unfortunate fish which become trapped. Size, 3 inches.

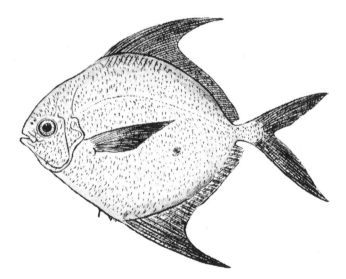

128. HARVESTFISH
Peprilus alepidotus

Also called Whiting.

Bluish above, silvery below. Takes a hook baited with bits of clam or crabmeat. Sometimes netted. The flavor is as rich and delicate as pompano and highly prized as a food fish. Size, 4 to 10 inches.

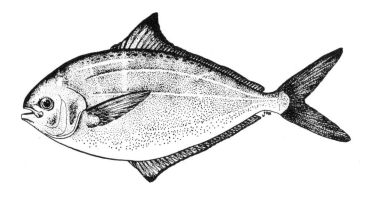

129. BUTTERFISH — *Peprilus triacanthus*

Also called Dollarfish, Sheepshead, Pumpkinseed, Starfish.
Usually abundant on the Atlantic coast in July. They seem to appear when the mackerel do. Size, 4 to 8 inches. Edibility, good.

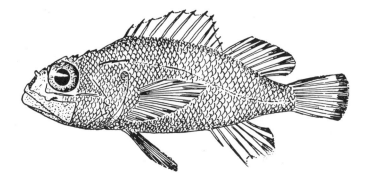

130. SMOOTHHEAD SCORPIONFISH — *Scorpaena calcarata*

Brownish above shading to a pinkish-red belly. Large brown spot above pectoral fin. Size, about 3 inches. One of four species of scorpionfishes found in the shrimp beds off Tortugas.

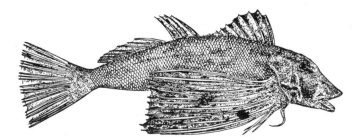

131. NORTHERN SEAROBIN   *Prionotus carolinus*

Ranges from Massachusetts to South America. Dark body with mottled spots. Though their wing-like fins suggest flying, they're bottom fish. The name "robin" may come from the singing sounds they produce through airbladders. The lower pectoral fins have developed into finger-like feelers with which they "walk" and probe the sand for food. Size, to 12 inches.

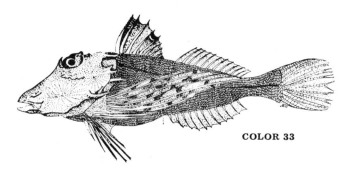

COLOR 33

132. BIGHEAD SEAROBIN   *Prionotus tribulus*

Occurs from North Carolina through the Gulf of Mexico. Of the many species of searobins, the Bighead is the one more often encountered close to shore in Florida waters. Has dark horizontal stripe. Rarely eaten in this country, but considered a delicacy in some areas.

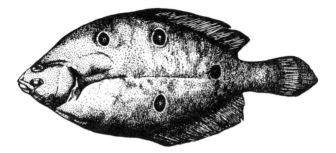

133. OCELLATED FLOUNDER   *Ancylopsetta quadrocellata*

Of the dozen or so flounders occurring in Florida, this is one of the most frequently caught. A left-eye flounder (eyes and coloration on left side of body) with several white-ringed dark spots. Size, around 10 inches. Edibility, good.

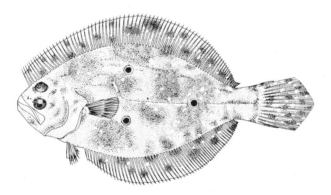

134. GULF FLOUNDER   *Paralichthys albigutta*

Has three dark-ringed spots forming a triangle; more pronounced in younger specimens. Color brownish. Often found over mud flats. Known to enter rivers. Average size, 10 or 12 inches. Food value, good.

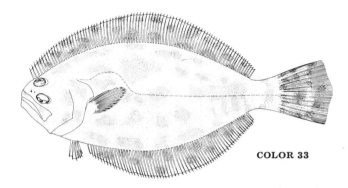

COLOR 33

135. SOUTHERN FLOUNDER   *Paralichthys lethostigma*

Much like the Gulf Flounder, which is found in the same area, except that the spots and blotches are more diffused and irregularly placed. Also good food.

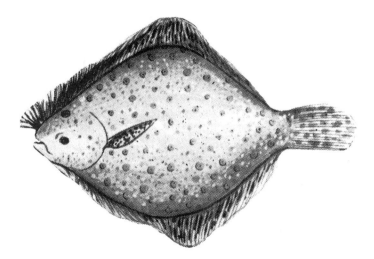

136. WINDOWPANE   *Scophthalmus aquosus*

Also called Sand Dab.

This is a small flounder, so thin that is possible to see light through the body. Perfectly camouflaged to resemble the coarse sand over which it is found. Edible, but contains so little meat that it's hardly worthwhile.

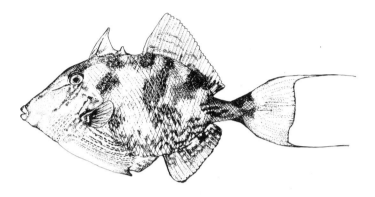

137. GRAY TRIGGERFISH   *Balistes capriscus*

Also called Leatherjack.

Gray, with darker markings. Preys on sea urchins. Hard armor-like scales. Size: to 12 inches. Food value: good.

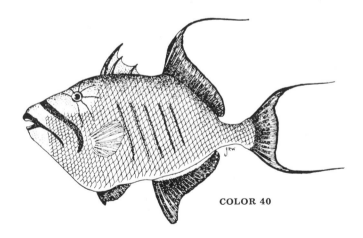

COLOR 40

138. QUEEN TRIGGERFISH   *Balistes vetula*

Grayish-blue upper body, yellowish belly. Two broad bluish-purple bands across snout, smaller blue stripes radiate from eye. Fins blue. Ranges from Massachusetts to Brazil. Size, 12 inches. Edible.

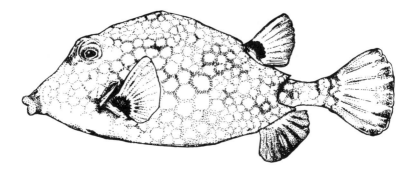

139. SMOOTH TRUNKFISH   *Lactophrys triqueter*

Hard shell-like covering on body — fairly common on offshore reefs. Feeds on crabs and worms which it routs from the sand, sometimes by ejecting a stream of water from the mouth. Light colored body with dark spots and bars. Seldom marketed, but they are good food. Size, 10 to 12 inches.

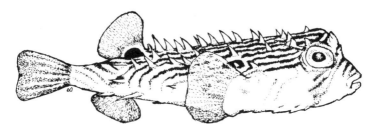

140. STRIPED BURRFISH   *Chilomycterus schoepfi*

Also called Spiny Boxfish, Porcupine Fish.

Belongs to the porcupinefish clan, and is inflatable like the puffers. Yellowish with brown stripes and thorn-like broad spines. Size, about 10 inches. Good aquarium fish.

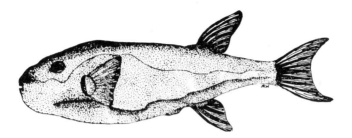

141. SMOOTH PUFFER   *Lagocephalus laevigatus*

Also called Rabbitfish.

Silvery with black blotches. Its four teeth, fused into a beak, are used to crush the shells of the crustaceans. Smooth, shiny skin with no scales; head shape suggests the name "rabbitfish." Most of those caught (on hook and line) average around 12 inches, but sometimes to 24 inches.

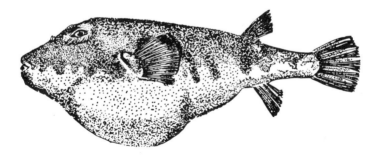

142. SOUTHERN PUFFER   *Sphoeroides nephelus*

Olive-brown color with light and dark bluish mottled splotches. One of the smaller puffers (10 inches) when uninflated, but swells to incredible size when disturbed. Most of the puffers are poisonous to some degree, but some species are eaten and regarded as excellent food.

INDEX — COMMON NAMES

INDEX — SCIENTIFIC NAMES

SALTWATER LICENSE REQUIRED
IN THE STATE OF FLORIDA

As of January 1, 1990, a saltwater fishing license is required for taking, attempting to take, or possessing marine fish from Florida waters.

The cost of the saltwater fishing license for Florida residents is $12 for a year and $10 for a 10-day license, plus a service charge. The cost for non-residents is $30 for a year, $15 for a 7-day, and $5 for a 3-day license, plus a service charge. Licenses may be purchased at county tax collector's offices and designated bait and tackle shops throughout the state. If you are a Florida resident and are certified as totally and permanently disabled, you are entitled to receive, without charge from the county tax collector, a permanent saltwater fishing license.

You must have a saltwater fishing license unless you meet one of the following exemptions:

- You are under the age of 16.

- You are a Florida resident fishing in saltwater from land or from a structure fixed to land.

- You are fishing from a boat that has a valid Vessel Saltwater Fishing License.

- You hold a valid saltwater products license, unless you are the owner, operator, or custodian of a vessel for which a saltwater fishing license is required.

- You are a Florida resident 65 years of age or older.

- You are a Florida resident, a member of the Armed Forces, are not stationed in Florida, and are home on leave for 30 days or less, with valid orders in your possession.

- You have been accepted by the Florida Department of Health and Rehabilitative Services for developmental services.

- You are fishing from a pier that has been issued a Pier Saltwater Fishing License.

- You have been assigned by a court to a Health and Rehabilitative Services authorized rehabilitation program involving training in Florida aquatic resources.

- You are a Florida resident fishing for mullet in freshwater and have a valid Florida freshwater fishing license.

- You are a Florida resident fishing for a saltwater species in freshwater from land or from a structure fixed to the land.